# TROUBLES
## Mastering your Pi

MW00785086

By Gabby Franco
Olympian, Firearms Instructor, Competitor and Author.

TroubleShooting by Gabby Franco

www.GabbyFranco.com

# ACKNOWLEDGMENTS

Special thanks to God for the great opportunities He has given to me and for the people He has brought to my Life. I am dreaming and achieving in faith.

Special thanks to my parents Maritza and Pascual because they inspire me to always fight for my dreams and because they introduced me to shooting sports. I am very grateful to have wonderful siblings Maru, Mariangel, and Pascual Daniel. Also thanks to my family in Miami: my cousin Peggy, Frank, Nina, and my Aunt Isidra. To my fiancé Johnathan and his family members who had helped me on this adventure, Glenn, Karen, Cliff, and Amber.

I would love to thank these friends who supported me in the shooting sports: My couches Guillermo and Otar, Elder, Plinio, Rory, John, Andy, Ronald, and the family of SFPC. Also huge thanks to my friends that supported me throughout this adventure: Cata, Angel, and Dr. Santos.

Special thanks to my friend and sponsor Brian from Mixon Targets for his unconditional support since the first day we talked about releasing this shooting manual.

Thank you to the editor Scott Olstead and photographers Fabiano Silva and Jaime Pacheco for their professionalism and great job on this book.

To my sponsors for believing in me and for their support: Black Rain Ordnance, Pistol Pay, Taran Tactical, TeludyneTech, and FrogLube.

And lastly, I also wish to thank all my friends, fans, followers, and students for all their LOVE. You keep me going!

TroubleShooting by Gabby Franco

www.GabbyFranco.com

# CONTENTS

TroubleShooting by Gabby Franco

# INTRODUCTION

designed this manual to help all levels of shooters master their shooting skills. I wrote it because I feel there are many people who need guidance when shooting. I believe that learning effective techniques in a friendly, easy-to-understand atmosphere will transform the way you shoot—you'll rise to a new and better level than you ever thought possible.

Whether you are a novice or an experienced shooter, *you should carry this manual in your range bag*. Why? Because even the most experienced shooters need to be reminded of the fundamentals from time to time.

From the moment you begin reading this manual you will note that I treat you like my student. So think of me as your coach. And as your coach, I will do my best to bring the best out of you by helping you improve your shooting skills to a higher level.

What's a marksman? A shooter who understands, perfects, and applies the fundamentals to any discipline of shooting he/she performs.

You must consider yourself a marksman before you label yourself as a tactical, practical (USPSA), defensive (IDPA), cowboy (SASS), or any other kind of shooter. At the end, what it all comes down to is your shooting skills and your ability to apply them to any shooting activity.

I was born in Venezuela, where I started shooting. About 20 years ago, my father introduced me to the shooting sports, specifically Olympic shooting in the disciplines of air pistol (.177 cal.) and sport pistol (.22 LR).

For 10 years, I dedicated my life to training six days a week for three to four hours every session. I traveled to 14 different countries, participated at national and international competitions and won several medals. One of my best achievements as an athlete was winning a silver medal at the Pan-American Games in Winnipeg, Canada, in 1999, which gave me a platform to go to the 2000 Olympic Games in Sydney, Australia. My last competition as an Olympic shooter was in Brazil at the South American Games in 2002, where I won three gold medals.

In 2002, I moved to the United States looking for a better life. I started working in the firearm industry; I sold firearms and accessories for six years, and I gained a lot of knowledge about different guns, parts, and popular customizations. Along with my job, I started shooting USPSA matches and learned some tactics.

During my life as an Olympic shooter, I had two wonderful coaches who taught me important techniques I still use today. They trained me as one of the best; and I became one of the best Olympic shooters in Venezuela. I trained hard, I never gave up.

## SHOOTING EXPERIENCE - 20 YEARS
1996 - 2001 - Venezuela National Champ - Air and Sport Pistol
1997 - Silver Medal — Bolivarian Games (Arequipa, Peru)
1998 - Silver Medal — Central American Games Maracaibo, Venezuela
1998 - Gold Medal — South American Games (Cuenca, Ecuador)
1999 - Silver Medal — Pan American Games (Winnipeg, Canada)
2000 - Olympic Games (Sydney, Australia)
2000 - Gold Medal — South American Games (Lima, Per)
2001 - Gold Medal — Bolivarian Games (Ambato, Ecuador)
2001 - 9TH Place — World Cup (Atlanta, GA USA)
2002 - 3 Gold Medals - S. American Games (Rio De Janeiro, Brazil)
2011 - Second Place - USPSA AREA 6 Frostproof, FL

## SHOOTING COURSES AND CERTIFICATIONS
- Tactical Pistol Training
- Tactical Carbine Training
- NRA Certified Pistol Instructor

- NRA Refuse to be a Victim Instructor
- Glock Professional Certified Armorer
- Season 4 TOP SHOT Contestant: First woman to reach the individual portion of the competition.
- Season 5 TOP SHOT "All Stars": Only woman to compete in the All Stars Show.

Today, my only goal as an instructor is making my students great shooters. So I won't give up on you, either! My expectation is that by reading this manual and using it regularly, you will shoot better than you ever have before. But you will carry out that feat only if you apply what I teach you here. So you need to open your eyes and your mind. Read, analyze and apply.

Not too long ago I participated at a local match in honor of veterans. I planned to shoot the pistol match only so I took my Glock 17 to the range. As I registered, a good friend who also had signed up for the match, approached me and asked me if I was planning to shoot the rifle event as well. I wasn't, but after talking to him for a while he changed my mind and I decided to shoot the rifle match with his firearm, which I had never seen or shot before. I figured since the match was just for fun I'd simply do the best I could.

Since he had competed in the previous relay, I wasn't able to check the rifle until it was my time to shoot. While I competed, my friend stood next to me at all times, telling me where to aim according to how he had zeroed his rifle. Not only was it the first time I had fired his gun, but it was the first time I had ever used a 1-4X rifle scope.

I fired from four positions at four distances:

    Prone: 100 Yards
    Sitting: 75 Yards
    Kneeling: 50 Yards
    Standing: 25 Yards.

I shot a 394 out of a possible maximum score of 400, including one shot on the 8-ring and four shots on the 9-ring. The rest of the rounds hit the 10 and X-ring.

The point is I want you to understand that no matter which firearm you have in your hands, no matter which discipline you are shooting, if you are a true marksman you should apply the fundamentals of shooting as perfectly as possible. Do that and you will give yourself a great opportunity to achieve a good place in any competition—or be the winner, as I was in this match.

# Sportsmanship
# Code of Conduct

- **READ**, know and follow ALL firearm safety rules.

- **GET TRAINED**, get educated and then practice responsibly. A well-educated gun owner is a better shooter.

- **USE YOUR FIREARMS RESPONSIBLY**. Whether you use them for self-defense, sporting purposes, or entertainment. Remember that every action has consequences; make sure you are aware of them.

- **Act in a Sportsman-like Manner** with respect towards others while in competitions and/or while training. Be a role model for your kids, family members and others. A good attitude goes a long way toward building a better reputation in the shooting sports, and it keeps our Second Amendment alive.

- **Be Aware** of gun laws in your area and follow them.

- **Store your Guns Safely**. They should never be left unattended. When not in use, they must be stored so they are not available to unauthorized people.

"Once you take control of a firearm, you are responsible for any accidents caused due to negligence"

-Gabby Franco

# CHAPTER 1
## Firearm Safety Rules

## TREAT ALL FIREARMS AS IF THEY ARE LOADED

1. When manipulating a firearm, always handle it as if it's loaded.
2. You must verify that the firearm is not loaded by checking that the magazine has been removed and the chamber is empty.

If someone hands you a firearm and assures you that it isn't loaded, you MUST verify the fact by looking into the chamber to make sure it is empty. It does not matter whether you trust the person; you can only trust yourself and what you verify visually and physically.

Remember: Once you take control of a firearm, you are responsible for any accidents caused due to negligence.

Do not rely on the "safety" mechanism of a firearm. Due to wear and sometimes faulty manufacturing, the safety may wear down or malfunction; it may not work properly.

## ALWAYS KEEP THE GUN POINTED IN A SAFE DIRECTION

Playing with a firearm is PROHIBITED. Pointing a firearm at people or anything other than a target, even in a playful way, breaks this rule and endangers lives and/or property.

Before you dry-fire a firearm, ALWAYS "*Treat your Firearm As If it is Loaded*."

## Keep Your Finger Off the Trigger

If you do not intend to fire the pistol you are handling, your finger(s) MUST be kept off the trigger and trigger guard area.

Keeping your finger off the trigger, even when handling, airsoft guns, plastic guns, etc., develops good habit that will prevent you from causing a possible accidental discharge (AD) while manipulating a loaded firearm.

## Be Sure of Your Target and What is Beyond It

Do not fire until you positively identify your target. Consider that the caliber you are firing might enable the bullet to continue traveling even after hitting your target; you must make sure that the bullet won't impact anything other than the target.

## Always Wear Eye and Ear Protection

Shooting glasses protect you from unexpected ricochet, powder residue, hot brass, and other undesired objects that can land in your eye area.

Ear muffs and/or ear plugs protect your hearing, which could be permanently damaged by the noise of your gun.

## Be Sure You Can Safely Operate a Firearm

Before taking it to the range, make sure your gun is in good condition and well-maintained, especially the barrel, which could have a buildup of corrosion and/or residue.

If the report and recoil of a fired cartridge is not normal, DO NOT FIRE AGAIN—you may have fired a round with less

14

powder, which can leave a bullet lodged in the barrel (a "squib load"). Unload your pistol, disassemble it, and inspect the barrel.

## VERIFY YOUR AMMUNITION

Be sure you have the correct ammunition for your handgun, confirm it by ensuring that the caliber printed on the ammo box matches the caliber printed on the following: factory pistol case, barrel, slide and the magazine(s).

Always use ammunition that comes from a trusted source such as: A gun shop, gun range, and/or a trusted online store.

If you handload your own ammunition, be sure to use the proper components and powder load for the caliber you are reloading.

*When unloading a firearm, ALWAYS remove the magazine first and then clear the chamber by moving or locking back the slide.*

# Semi-Auto Pistol

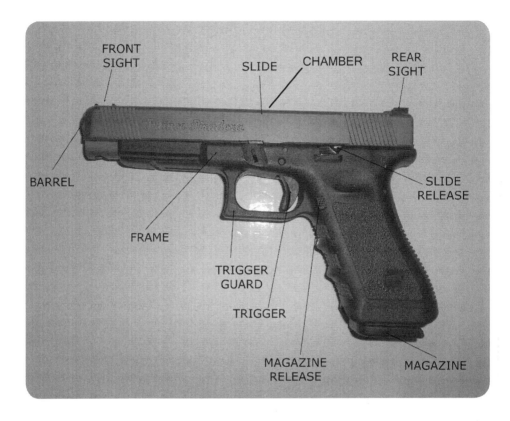

FRONT SIGHT, SLIDE, CHAMBER, REAR SIGHT, BARREL, SLIDE RELEASE, FRAME, TRIGGER GUARD, TRIGGER, MAGAZINE RELEASE, MAGAZINE

A semi-auto pistol is a handgun that fires one round with every trigger pull, ejects and extracts the empty shell, and then loads the next round until the magazine is empty.

Some semi-automatic pistols have external hammers. Ex: Sig Sauer, CZ, H&K, FNH, 1911, etc. And some others are firing pin operated (no external hammer) as the picture above. Ex: Glock, Springfield XD, S&W M&P9, Kahr, etc.

Rounds are feed automatically into the chamber with a single stack magazine (7-10 rounds) or double stack magazines (12rds or more) after each shot.

# REVOLVERS

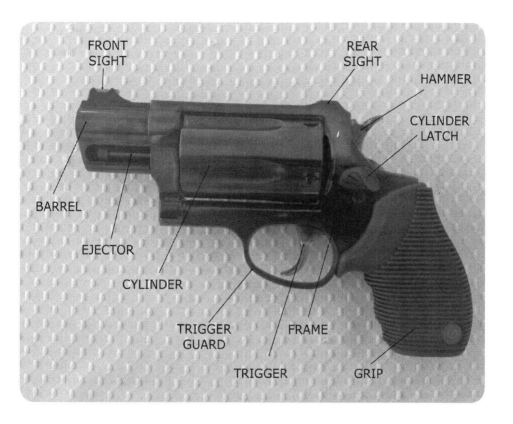

A revolver is a handgun that has a cylinder which rotates to align each round with the firing mechanism (hammer) and barrel as the shooter squeeze the trigger.

After the shooter fires all rounds in the cylinder, he/she needs to manually remove the empty shells using the ejector located below the barrel.

Depending on the size of the frame and/or caliber of the revolver, they may hold between 5 to 10 rounds in the cylinder.

www.GabbyFranco.com

# CHAPTER 2
## SHOOTING TECHNIQUES

Imagine that you have never played tennis in your life and I give you a tennis racquet and I tell you to play with me. Of course you might have seen tennis on TV, and you probably have seen some people doing it before but you have never done it in the past. As soon as we start playing you will probably hit the ball a few times instinctively (just because you can swing the racquet with your arm), and with a lot of luck you might be able to make a point. But you look clumsy to spectators, and they definitely know that you don't know how to play tennis.

You have no technique whatsoever.

The same philosophy applies to shooting. Just because you can pull the trigger and randomly hit a target doesn't mean you know how to properly shoot a firearm. Your target shows the lack of technique.

Let's solve that problem.

# DOMINANT EYE

The dominant eye not only transmits information faster to your brain but also is the one that focuses on the target and guides the movement of your other eye. By determining the dominant eye you will be able to shoot more comfortably, and with training you will be able to shoot with both eyes open effectively. Why? Because your dominant eye will focus clearly, leaving the other eye to "fill in the gaps" of the image.

Be aware that your dominant eye might not be on your dominant side. You can be right-handed and left-eye dominant, or left-handed and right eye dominant *(See Fig. 2)*.
Therefore, you cannot assume you are right-eye dominant because you are right-handed.

Important: Keep your head in a straight vertical position. By tilting your head you will have the tendency to twist your upper torso.

How to determine eye dominance:
* Pick a spot in front of you about 7 to 10 feet away.
* Put your hands together in front of you, making a triangle by overlapping both hands; extend your arms.
* With both eyes open, look at your target through the open space between your hands.
* Bring your hands towards your face.
* Your hands will lie over your dominant eye.

Another way to find your eye dominance is by cutting a relatively small hole in a piece of paper.
* Look at your target through the open space on the paper with both eyes open.
* Bring the paper to your face.
* Paper will lie over your dominant eye.

*Are you a cross-dominant person? Are you right-handed but left eye-dominant, or vice versa? Well, don't worry: It is really not a big deal. What you need to do is align the sights to your eyes, not your face to your sights.*

Right-Hand shooter - Right eye dominant

Right-Hand shooter - Left eye dominant

# SHOOTING STANCE

Just as it is with the rest of the techniques taught in this manual, the stance you use is very important to shoot proficiently.

A proper stance will help you to:

1) Control the recoil of your firearm.
2) Have better balance as you shoot, even on the move.
3) Shoot for long periods of time more efficiently.

I have created an acronym for you to remember easily: *LATCH*
It stands for: Legs, Arms, Torso, Chin and Hands.

## LEGS

### Bend your knees:

In order to keep your chest forward without losing your balance, you need to bend your knees a bit and in a comfortable way without compromising the technique. Over-doing it will cause fatigue and muscle strain. Your legs will work like shock-absorbers whether shooting on the move (tactical, USPSA, IDPA, etc.) or while shooting from a stationary position (target shooting).

### Strong leg, slightly back:

For a more balanced stance, move your dominant leg slightly back; this will give you extra stability. If you are a right-handed shooter, your dominant leg is your right leg. Use shoulder width as a reference for the distance between your feet.
*(See Fig. 3 on Page 23).*

Fig. 3

POSITION

Shooting position of a Right Hand shooter:  Knees slightly bended and right leg slightly back for extra support.

## Natural point of aim:

You must square up to the target. That is, you must face the target in a way that guarantees your body resides in a natural position.

Remember that the rest of your body will follow your head and your feet. This is known as establishing your natural point of aim.

Shooting every day is not always and option, however you do not need to retrain your body how to stand while shooting; so establishing a natural point of aim helps you to begin each training session using what your body already knows.

Square up to objects, people, etc., is something we naturally do throughout our daily activities. Some examples of natural body positions used in non-shooting activities are:

* Talking to someone; your face is straight looking at the eyes of the other person.
* Sitting at a table to eat, to write, or to work on a computer.
* Looking at detail an object such as a painting.

Note: This principle doesn't apply to every shooting activity we do, but in this case we use it because it works well with pistol shooting.

Example: A right-handed shooter has both feet pointing to the right as shown on *Fig. 5* (page 25), and his/her chest pointing toward the target. This stance would allow one to shoot, however it is not a consistent position, because the angle on which the feet are pointed may change from session to session.

In the other hand, shooting with your body squared up to the target as shown on *Fig. 4* (Page 25) allows you to shoot with consistency and accuracy.

*Note: Techniques change within the different shooting disciplines.*

*Students always ask me: Shouldn't I try a different shooting stance? My answer is: A shooter should always experiment and try different stances (example: a weaver stance) and always keep in mind that all will allow you to shoot, but the shooting stance I explained will maximize your abilities.*

In the picture below you can see two different shooting stances. On left *(Fig. 4)* is the shooting position I recommend.

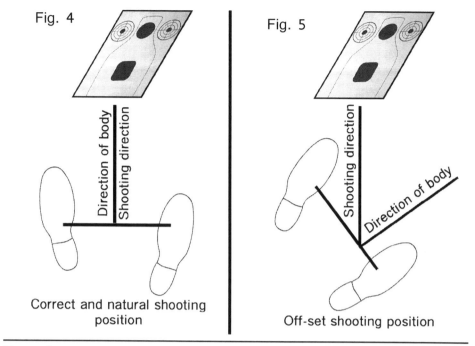

Fig. 4 — Correct and natural shooting position

Fig. 5 — Off-set shooting position

## Exercise:

No firearm required. Ask someone to read the exercise for you.
Read all 4 steps first.

1. Using *Fig. 5* as a reference, aim at a wall or target with your hands together as if you were holding a pistol.
2. Close your eyes and breathe deeply.
3. Keep your eyes closed and then put your hands down. Relax your arms on each side of your body and breathe again. (Keep your eyes closed).
4. Lift your hands again as if you were aiming with your pistol, breathe deeply for the last time, and then open your eyes.

As you can see, your body is aiming off the target. Your body adjusts itself to a natural position.

Repeat the same exercise with the stance in *Fig. 4*. Notice that even with your eyes closed you can acquire your target quickly and easily.

# Arms and Shoulders

## Shoulders:

Keep shoulders in a natural position while you shoot, similar to the way you walk around and behave in a normal environment.

Rolling your shoulders too much and raises them too high (almost to the same level of your ears), will cause your arms and muscles to be tense transmitting the recoil stress to your neck and bottom of your head, creating muscle fatigue that will make you feel tired faster. This mistake is commonly done by shooters due to a false sensation of control over the firearm.

---

Exercise:

### No firearm required

1. Stand on front of a wall and imagine you are holding a pistol.
2. Aim at the wall or target, put the same pressure on your shoulder and upper back as you normally do while shooting.
3. Analyze the tension and the stress on your muscles.
4. Lower your hands, you are about to repeat the exercise again.
5. Put your hands at eye level without putting stress on your shoulders.
6. Feel how it's a more natural, relaxed, and enjoyable shooting position.

This is how you will shoot from now on. *Trust me, it works better.*

*Another downside of tensing up your shoulders is that you will start anticipating every shot. Even if you are a great shooter, your rounds will land in the lower part of the bullseye or otherwise too low on the target. Remember to keep the shoulder and upper back firm but not too stiff. Just relax, and try to find the perfect balance.*

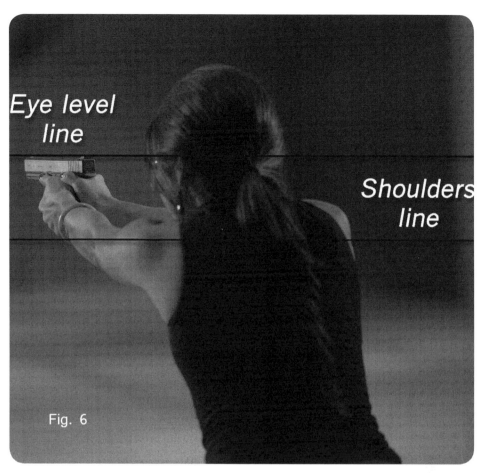

Position must be as natural as possible

## Arms straight:

There are different techniques concerning the proper position of your arms and elbow. I recommend to keep your arms straight without hyper-extending them to avoid muscle fatigue. Elbows play an important role to increase your shooting speed and recoil control as I will explain next.

The position I recommend is Elbows out. See *Fig. 8* (page 29).

## Position 1, Elbows In:

Your arms are extended normally. Using this technique, your elbows are less exposed allowing you to bring them closer to your body when shooting behind cover or in a tactical scenario. It is an instinctive position. However, your elbows will slightly bend upward due to recoil. This will make you feel like you need to keep your elbows locked and/or engage different muscles to keep it from happening.

Fig. 7

## Position 2, Elbows Out:

While aiming at the target, rotate your elbows outwards. This is a good option for more effective and faster shooting. You will feel a slight pressure on the inside of your shoulders and arms; that's normal if this is the first time you do it.

This technique will send the recoil of the pistol in a straight line back, helping you recover your sights a lot faster and more consistently. Your arms are not hyper-extended and your elbows are not bended either. Always keep arms extended in a natural and comfortable position.

Fig. 8

This technique will send the recoil of the pistol in a straight line back

## Exercise:

At the range with loaded firearm; make sure your *finger is off the trigger until ready to shoot.*

1. Load your firearms with 5 rounds
2. Aim at the target with your "elbows in" *See Fig. 7* (page 28) and fire all 5 rounds consecutively with a controlled speed.
3. Repeat the same exercise, with your "elbows out". *See Fig. 8* (page 29)

During the first 5-rounds (elbows in) your position is natural and easy to execute; however, you feel the need to lock your arms and shoulders to keep the front sight in place.

During the second set of 5 rounds (elbows out), your elbows cannot bend up, which gives you more muzzle control; allowing you to recover your front sight more easily and faster.

# Torso

You must lean forward to change the center of gravity of your body. Putting more body weight toward the target creates a natural resistance to the recoil of the handgun. It is important that your stance is solid but not tense (tensing up will cause anticipation of each shot); keep your muscles relaxed. Accept the recoil of the pistol, don't fight it.

As you see in the next pictures *(Fig. 9 and Fig. 10)*, the body appears balanced. As you become more comfortable with this technique, I encourage you to go a bit more aggressive in coordination with your legs, especially when you start increasing the shooting speed.

*Many shooters mistakenly try to control recoil by tensing their bodies while leaning forward, resulting in entire groups of low impacts. Of course you must lean forward a bit, but do not tense up while you do it.*

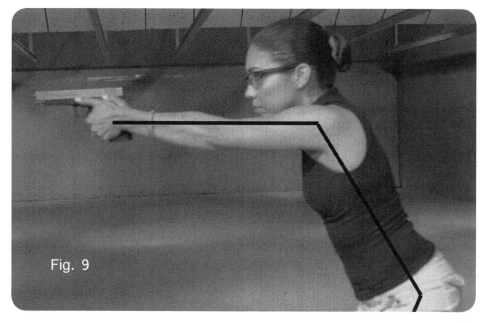

Fig. 9

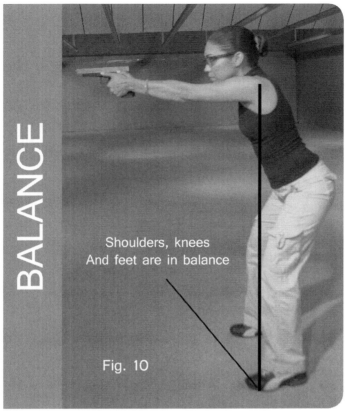

BALANCE

Shoulders, knees
And feet are in balance

Fig. 10

Position of Shoulders and Knees is Balanced.

## Exercise:

No firearm required

1. Stand with both arms extended as if you were aiming.
2. Tell a friend to *gently* tap five consecutive times on your knuckles (simulating the recoil of the firearm).
   - Notice how balanced you are as you bend your knees while your chest is forward.
3. Repeat the exercise, but now, tell your friend to inadvertently stop his hand just before he taps your knuckles (between the second and fifth tap).
   - If you move forward, you are anticipating; you're too tense.
4. Repeat this exercise without tension until you don't anticipate the simulated recoil.

# CHIN AND FACE

Wherever your head goes your body follows. We know this instinctively because it is how our body works—we don't think about it. If you want to turn your body to the right the first thing you do is turn your head in that direction, then your body will follow. We must apply the same principle while shooting.

In order to maintain a chest-forward stance as mentioned before, you must bring your chin and face toward the target, forcing your chest to stay in the position desired. You will find great benefits by using this technique; you will also use it to shoot firearms like shotguns and rifles.

> *Note: Keep your chin in a natural position. Try not to move it up or down because this will change the point of impact (See Fig. 11). Moving your chin up to see over the sights of your pistol causes your shots to string vertically. Keeping your chin tucked in reduces your peripheral vision and the frames of your glasses might interfere with the sight alignment.*

Fig. 11

## Exercise:

1. Facing a wall, stand with your hands down and relaxed.
2. Move your head towards the wall as if you want to touch it.
3. Notice how your chest tries to move forward as well.

To avoid changes in point of impact you must not exaggerate this movement. Don't over-extend the muscles of your neck when you move with your chin forward. All your movements must be as natural as possible.

# HANDS

Your hands play a critical role while shooting. Instinctively, you will tend to keep a very tight grip with your dominant hand (what some call a "death grip"), giving you a false sense of security and control over the firearm. But keep in mind your hands should work as a team. Like any team, each member has its own responsibility.

Generally the fingers of your hands work together at all the times. Every time you grab something, all five fingers interact in one way or another to do the task. This is something we need to control, especially with our dominant hand. The only finger that needs to move is the trigger finger.

## Dominant hand

This hand must have a firm grip but it must not squeeze the pistol very hard. This hand holds the trigger finger, which should work only to squeeze the trigger perfectly. *Dominant hand pressure is about 30 percent.*

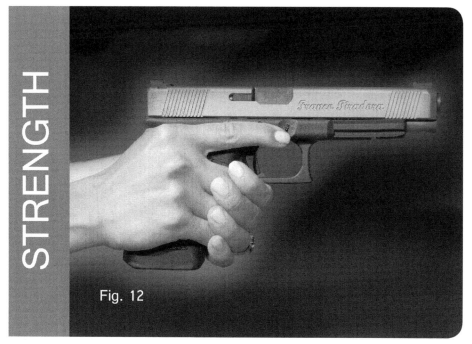

Fig. 12

## Keep a high grip:

Keep your dominant hand as high as possible on the pistol grip, leaving no space between your hand and the top of it as shown on Fig. 13. This will help you control and recover your sight picture a lot faster; it will also prevent you from limp-wristing every time you shoot.

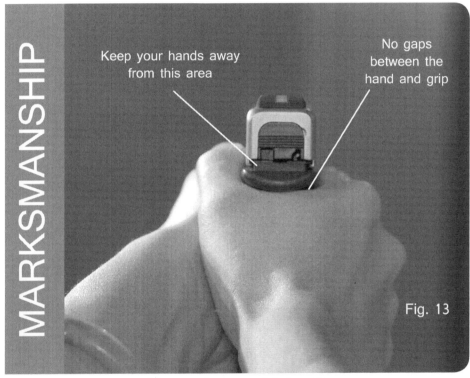

Always keep a high grip

Important:

As you know the slide of a semi-automatic pistol moves all the way back every time you squeeze the trigger to load the next round; that is why you need to keep your hand away from the path of the slide to avoid injuries.

36

## Exercise:

No firearm required

1. Close your hand tightly into a fist.
2. While keeping the same pressure on all fingers, move your index finger only and analyze such movement. It doesn't move smoothly, does it?
   - Moving your trigger finger while your entire hand is applying a "death grip" to the pistol will not allow you to squeeze the trigger smoothly.

3. Now close your hand with light pressure.
4. As in the previous exercise, move your index finger.
   - As you can see, your finger moves more freely and even faster than before.

You will do yourself a favor by keeping a *firm* grip with your dominant hand that is *not very tight*.

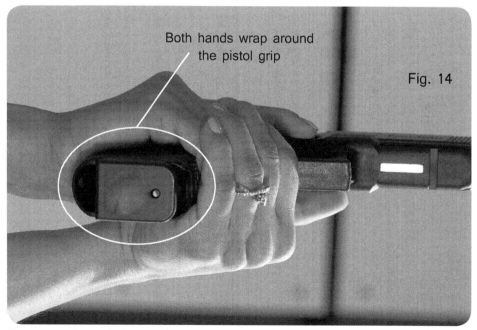

Both hands wrap around the pistol grip

Fig. 14

<u>Support hand</u> fingers are almost perfectly aligned and they cover the dominant hand fingers.

## Support hand

Your support hand must stay firm with a strong grip (to a level of comfort) with about 70 percent pressure. Lock your wrist and maintain a more pronounced angle for a better muzzle control of the handgun. *See Fig. 15.*

- In order to have a strong/high grip and good wrist angle, keep your fingers under the trigger guard as shown in the *Fig. 17.*
- Your thumb must point straight to the target and remain parallel to the barrel of the pistol. *See Fig. 15, 16.*

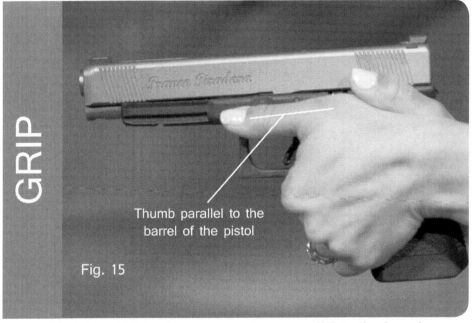

GRIP

Thumb parallel to the barrel of the pistol

Fig. 15

Thumbs point at the target and are parallel to the barrel

*Another way to keep your support hand high enough is to make sure your index finger (of such hand) touches the bottom part of the trigger guard. If you feel the trigger guard, then it means you are having a good grip. See Fig. 17.*

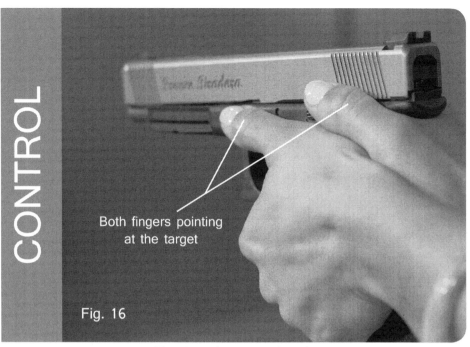

CONTROL

Both fingers pointing at the target

Fig. 16

No gaps between hands

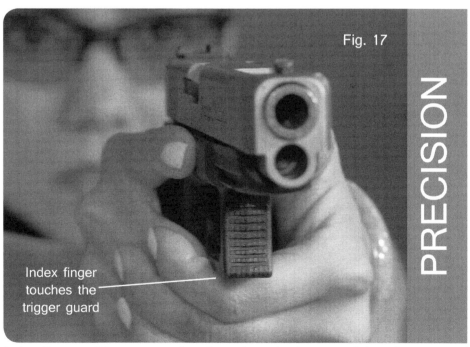

PRECISION

Fig. 17

Index finger touches the trigger guard

Index finger of the support hand touches the bottom of the trigger guard

## In-line grip:

As shown on *Fig. 19*, the pistol is completely aligned with the arm of your dominant hand to help you acquire a natural point of aim. This is the correct way to grip a pistol.

- The entire lower palm and the thenar muscle (part of the thumb) receives the impact of the recoil of the firearm. This is one aspect that is often taken for granted.

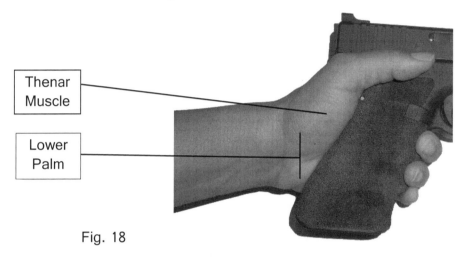

Thenar Muscle

Lower Palm

Fig. 18

- Your dominant hand must naturally grip the pistol from the rear without extending your trigger finger too far forward.

Fig. 19

Pistol in-line with wrist and arm

## Exercise: (At home)

Make sure firearm is unloaded. Keep your finger off the trigger

1.  Grip the pistol with your dominant hand only, as you normally do.
2.  Aim at the wall.
3.  Without taking your eyes off the wall and maintaining the same grip, lower your hand parallel to your leg, and relax your wrist.
4.  Now look down at your pistol and see if your gun is pointing straight down or the muzzle is more towards one side (left or right).

*   If the pistol is pointing straight down you have a good grip.
*   If the pistol is pointing to the side, your trigger finger is way too far forward, and you need to re-adjust your grip. (Ex: A right hand shooter might see his pistol pointing to the right instead of straight down).

*Make sure you apply all the techniques discussed before. I want you to shoot great, but to do that you need to keep your mind and eyes open to experiment all the techniques I have taught you in this shooting manual.*

*Consider that changing the way you normally shoot might not make you shoot better right away. Remember, I am teaching your body a new way of doing things, it might take a little bit of time for you to get used to it, but it will be worth it. Trust me!*

# PRACTICE DRILLS
## Shooting Position

www.GabbyFranco.com

Perfecting your body position is very important because it will help you be more consistent and will also maximize your abilities. Shooting, like any other sport, requires you to have a solid and firm position but not too stiff to avoid fatigue that lead to poor results during a practice session and/or competition.

Practice these drills every day or until you feel that your body is getting use to the new shooting position.

Before stepping on the line of fire, make sure you stretch. You are not running a marathon, but you will be using muscles that might be tense due to stress; I want all those muscles to be relaxed and warm. Warm muscles allow you to move smoothly because you will be relaxed, so your shooting session will be enjoyable.

Once you are ready at the shooting range and you have your pistol set to shoot, do five (5) to ten (10) dry-fires to help your mind transition from what you were doing at work, home, etc., to what you are about to do.

Spend quality time at the range by practicing perfect technique or as perfectly as possible, so your body can memorize good habits—what is known as muscle memory. Every time you shoot, you should be able to know what you did right or wrong at the moment you squeezed the trigger. If it is not clear, you must learn what went wrong by a process of elimination. Check on possible mistakes and errors. Keep a range log to record progress *(Use page 46)*.

# PRACTICE DRILLS
## DEFINING POSITION

---

<u>Round Count</u>: 15
<u>Distance</u>: 7 yards
<u>Shooting Hand</u>: Dominant
<u>Rate of Fire</u>: Slow
<u>Frequency</u>: Every day at the beginning of your training session until the position becomes natural.

    <u>First Five Rounds</u>: Concentrate on your legs, knees and feet. Make sure your feet face the target and your knees are bent comfortably; do not squat. While firing these five rounds, think about your comfort: Do you need to adjust this position by leaning more forward?

    <u>Second Five Rounds</u>: Focus on your shoulders. Aim at the target with your pistol without putting pressure on them. Relax the muscles of your back and inhale and exhale deeply in order to remain relaxed. If you feel you are putting more pressure on your shoulders again, do not fire; put the gun down. Prepare again to make another shot while concentrating on your shoulders.

    <u>Third Five Rounds</u>: Focus on your arms, which shouldn't be locked and tense. Remember, *the more naturally and relaxed you shoot, the better results you will get on the target*.

NOTES: _____

_____

_____

_____

_____

# PRACTICE DRILLS
## GRIP

---

Round Count: 10
Distance: 7 yards
Shooting Hand: Dominant
Rate of Fire: Slow
Frequency: Every day at the beginning of your training session until the position becomes natural.

1. Load your pistol with five rounds.
2. Put the gun down after each shot (this is not a rapid fire practice).
3. Verify that your hands are positioned correctly and thumbs are pointing forward.
4. Relax your dominant hand to the point where it feels a little bit loose.
5. Your support hand should have more pressure over your dominant hand.
6. Look at the angle of your wrist of your support hand; it must be pronounced.
7. Repeat the exercise.

If you need to fire more rounds to practice this technique feel free to do so, but do not exceed 20 rounds. The next day at the range, with a fresh mind, practice this drill again.

NOTES: _____
_____
_____
_____
_____
_____

# **P**RACTICE **D**RILLS
## TEST 1

(To be used after concentrating on body position for three days)

---

**Round Count**: 10 rounds
**Distance**: 7 yards
**Shooting Hand**: Dominant
**Rate of Fire**: Slow
**Frequency**: Once a week

1. Lay the pistol on the table *unloaded* and face down range.
2. Take the pistol from the table faster than normal and aim at the target (Keep finger off the trigger).
3. While aiming at the target, check every aspect of your position: Legs, Arms, Torso, Chin, and Hands.
4. Make sure the position of your body is in harmony—not too much, not too little.
5. Repeat steps 1, 2 and 3 with your pistol loaded (10 rounds).
6. After you check your position and you are certain that everything is correct, fire all 10 rounds.

Below write down the mistakes you made once you took the pistol from the table so you know what aspects of your shooting stance you need to work on more closely.

NOTES: _____

_____

_____

_____

_____

_____

_____

NOTES: _____

_____

_____

_____

_____

_____

_____

Mark or highlight your shot group to analyze your shooting technique.

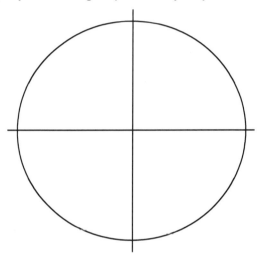

Make copies of this page

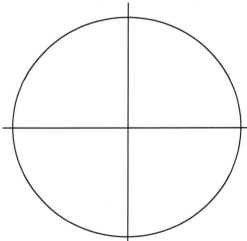

# Breathing Techniques

If you did not breathe you could not live. You do it so naturally you don't even realize how you do it, the intensity, or quality of it. You just breathe. Shooting, like other sports, is not exempt from using effective breathing techniques to assure adequate oxygen to your muscles; especially your eyes.

Inhaling and exhaling at least three (3) times before you start shooting will send oxygen to you blood. It will also help you with your concentration when you're tense or nervous.

During your shooting practice, breathing control is a crucial factor that must be considered, and here are a few techniques:

## Sniper Style:

Shooter exhales almost all the air in the lungs leaving about 20 percent of oxygen and immediately performs a shot. According to this technique, this is the moment when your body is the most relaxed and the muscles of your thorax are not stressed.

## Standard Hold:

Shooter maintains short but consistent breathing cycles while acquiring point of aim. Once on target and the process of aiming starts, the shooter exhales 40 percent of the air in the lungs or when the chest feels relaxed, and then holds the remaining air while performing a shot. The shooter fully exhales at the end of each shot.

## Belly Breathing:

Shooter breathes through the stomach and pushes out about 60 percent of the air in the lungs with it.

## Exercise:

<u>Firearms must be unloaded; use the "standard hold" breathing technique</u>

1. Inhale deeply.
2. Take aim at the target with your unloaded pistol.
3. Exhale about 40 percent of the air in your lungs or to the point your chest feels relaxed; then hold your breath.
4. Keep looking at the front sight as if you are going to shoot.
5. While holding your breath, start squeezing the trigger.

Analyze your pistol movement against your target. Notice that your body moves slower than before helping you during the aiming process.

After each trigger squeeze, exhale the rest of the air in your lungs and start the exercise again.

Important: For more effective results, do not hold your breath for more than 9 seconds, after that your body begins to display the effects of oxygen deficiency.

Remember that your eyes are the first part of your body to lose oxygen. The "standard hold" technique is very effective because it minimizes movement of your lungs while making a precision shot with a pistol. Feel free to try the other breathing techniques.

*When it comes to target shooting, you want your body in harmony—you want consistency and minimal movement. Out of all the different techniques explained, I use the "standard hold" because it prevents recoil anticipation, and keeps a steady and consistent body movement while aiming.*

# SIGHT ALIGNMENT

Sight alignment happens when the top of the front sight and the top of the rear sight are at the same level. This alignment is not complete until the front sight is in the middle of the rear sight's notch as seen on *Fig. 19 and Fig. 21.*

You could squeeze the trigger perfectly, have a perfect body stance, etc., but if you don't have a perfect sight alignment you won't hit where you aimed.

With practice you could also know where the bullet hit the target without looking at it—up, down, left, right— just by focusing on the front sight only, not on the target.

## Rear Sight:

Is on the back of the slide. Because the rear sight is the closest object to your eyes, you will see it very defined. You must not focus on it; the rear sight must stay blurry in your vision.

Fig. 19

Rear Sight

Rear sight must remain blurry in your vision.

## Front Sight:

The front sight is the only part of the firearm you should focus on, to make a perfect shot.

Perhaps you think you can see the front sight and the target simultaneously, or you wonder why your shot group is wide even though you are looking at the front sight every time you shoot. Whichever is your concern, you must remember that your eyes can focus on one object at a time, so if you are looking at the target you are not focusing on the front sight. This error is commonly done by beginners and some experience shooters; they take for granted the importance of the front sight. As you see on page 53, your sight alignment determines how close or wide your shot groups will be.

> *Please note that if you are shifting your attention from the front sight to the target, or from the front sight to the rear sight, then you won't be able to guarantee a perfect sight alignment. You must focus on the front sight only.*
> *The target and the rear sight must stay blurry.*

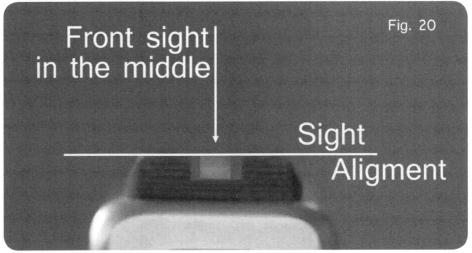

Sight alignment

## Exercise 1:

1. Place a pencil on a table (one end of it is the rear sight "**A**"; the other end is the front sight "**B**").
2. In front of the pencil place a small object (to simulate a target).
3. Place your left thumb on point A and with the other hand move B sideways. In order to keep the pen perfectly aligned to the simulated target, you need to make sure that A and B are perfectly perpendicular to it.

As you can see, the front sight is a super-important part of the process of shooting. On this exercise, **A** remains in a fixed position and only **B** moves. It doesn't matter how concentrated on the target you are; if you don't verify that **B** (front sight) is pointing at it, your shot will be off-center.

If you don't look at your front sight you won't hit the target as precisely as you want because your shots will always be a bit right or left. Most casual shooters think that to hit the bullseye they have to look at the target even for a little while, but that won't work.

After positively identifying your target, your eyes must look at the sights and start the process of sight alignment. While aiming, your rear and front sight move simultaneously due to different factors: Pulse, internal body movement, lung movement while inhaling and exhaling (depending on technique), stance, etc. Therefore, utmost attention must be given to sight alignment.

Switching your attention back and forth from the front sight to the target will make your eyes tired and it will be harder for you to focus; you will end up looking at the target and not at the front sight, resulting in a wide group of shots.

## Exercise 2:

1. Grab a pen with letters printed in it.
2. Facing your target, raise your hand, and put the pen between your eyes and the target.
3. Read what is written on the pen; check every detail, the letters and the color of the pen.
4. Now, with your peripheral vision, check the target. It is blurry, right? That is how the target should look if you focus on the front sight only.

Do not use the dots on the sights of your pistol as a guide—that will unconsciously make you switch your focus back and forth from the front sight to the rear sight. Instead, concentrate on how the top of both sight look aligned.

> *If you want to shoot in the bullseye, then you must make sure your sights are perfectly aligned.*

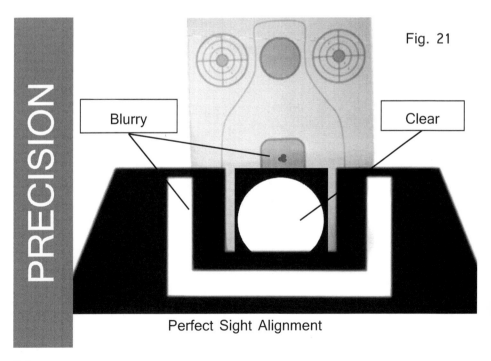

Fig. 21

Blurry

Clear

PRECISION

Perfect Sight Alignment

# RESULTS OF WRONG SIGHT ALIGNMENT

Before you judge the quality and sights of your firearm, be sure that you are not making any of these common mistakes.

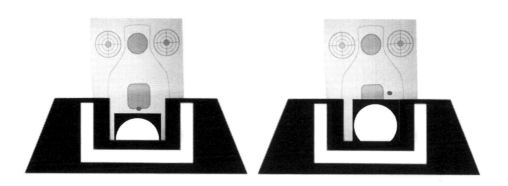

Low                              Right

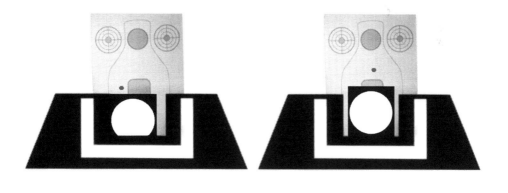

Left                              High

The shooting targets I recommend are Mixon Targets
www.mixontargets.com

# PRACTICE DRILLS
## Sight Alignment

www.GabbyFranco.com

You might wonder why in the next practice drills I say that "target results are not important", and I don't blame you, I wondered the same thing 15 years ago when my coach told me that. He explained to me that most shooters look at the target after each shot looking for the impact, and they forget that the most important thing about shooting is to trust the front sight: *Before, during and after each shot*.

Technique is more important than results.  Once you master the technique, results become irrelevant. Before you see your target, you know where your shot landed.

Before stepping on the line of fire, make sure you stretch. You are not running a marathon, but you will be using muscles that might be tense due to stress; I want all those muscles relaxed and warm. Warm muscles allow you to move smoothly because you will be more relaxed so your shooting session will be more enjoyable. Once you are ready at the shooting range and you have your pistol set to shoot, remind yourself to do five to 10 dry-fires to help your mind transition from what you were doing at work, home, etc., to what you are about to do. Prepare your mind by thinking about your shooting technique.

These are just a few simple exercises that will help you with concentration while shooting, to learn about shooting fundamentals, and to notice possible mistakes.

Check on possible mistakes and errors. Make notes.

# PRACTICE DRILLS
## SIGHT PICTURE 1

Round Count: 24
Distance: 7 yards
Shooting Hand: Dominant
Rate of Fire: Slow
Frequency: Every day at the beginning of your training session until the technique becomes natural.

1. Use any Mixon target of your preference.
2. During this drill, target results are not very important; concentrate on a perfect sight alignment.
3. Make sure you have a good stance and good grip *(Pages 22-41)*.
4. Load your pistol with 12 rounds only.
5. Fire three rounds in a row and **do not** look at the target after each shot. Keep your concentration on the front sight at all times before, during, and after each shot. Finish all 12 rounds.
6. Make sure the target is blurry.
7. If you caught yourself looking at the target, then as you shoot think about the technique: "Look at the front sight only"
8. Repeat this exercise twice.

By doing this exercise regularly you will be able to know whether you saw the front sight clearly or whether your eyes shifted from time to time between your sight picture and the target.
Write down if you were able to concentrate on the front sight only.

NOTES: _____
_____
_____
_____

# PRACTICE DRILLS
## SIGHT PICTURE 2

Round Count: 20 rounds
Distance: 10 yards
Target: White/plain; no bullseye or dots.
Shooting Hand: Dominant
Rate of Fire: Slow
Frequency: Every day at the beginning of your training session until the technique becomes natural.

Use a target with no bullseye, basically a white/plain paper. During this drill, target results are not very important; concentrate on a perfect sight alignment. Forget about the target and how good or bad you are shooting. Make sure you have a good stance and good grip *(Pages 22-41)*.

1. Load your pistol with 5 rounds.
2. Aim at the middle of the target (point of aim).
3. Make sure the target is blurry and your eyes are not shifting between the target and the front sight.
4. If you note that you looked at the target, then put the gun down. Prepare for the next shot thinking about the technique: "Look at the front sight only"
5. Repeat this exercise until you fire 20 rounds.

Write down if the group of shots are tight or not and where in the target are they concentrated: Up, down, down-left, etc.

NOTES: _____

_____

_____

_____

_____

# PRACTICE DRILLS
## SIGHT PICTURE 3

Round Count: 20
Distance: 15-20 yards
Target: Bullseye
Shooting Hand: Dominant
Rate of Fire: Slow
Frequency: Every day at the beginning of your training session until the technique becomes natural.

During this drill, target results are not very important; concentrate on a perfect sight alignment. Make sure you have a good stance and good grip *(Pages 22-41).*

1. Use any Mixon target of your preference.
2. Load your pistol with 10 rounds.
3. Fire two rounds in a row without looking where your shot hit the target. Finish all 10 rounds.
4. If you note that you looked at the target, then put the gun down. Prepare for the next shot thinking about the technique: "Look at the front sight only".
5. The front sight might cover the target; which is fine. Remember, this it is an optical effect; your front sight looks larger because it is closer to your eyes.
6. Dry fire 10 times to refresh the technique.
7. Repeat the exercise.

As you start shooting at greater distance, it is imperative that you look at the front sight more intensively, otherwise your shots won't be near the bullseye.

Using page 59, describe your shot group and indicate where your shots landed up, down, down-left, etc.

TroubleShooting by Gabby Franco                                          57

# PRACTICE DRILLS
## SIGHT PICTURE 4

**Round Count**: 20
**Distance**: 15-20 yards
**Target**: Bullseye
**Shooting Hand**: Dominant
**Rate of Fire**: Slow
**Extras**: Timer
**Frequency**: As many times as you feel necessary; exercise will help you concentrate on sight alignment.

During this exercise you will aim at the target for 30 seconds; then you will squeeze the trigger.

1. Set the timer for 30 seconds.
2. Aim at the target with your loaded pistol, and during the time maintain focus on the front sight only.
3. When the timer goes off you can shoot one shot only.
4. Repeat the exercise until you finish all 20 rounds.

Focus on the front sight must be perfect even after each shot.

NOTES: _____

_____

_____

_____

_____

_____

_____

_____

_____

NOTES: _____

_____

_____

_____

_____

_____

_____

Mark or highlight your shot group to analyze your shooting technique

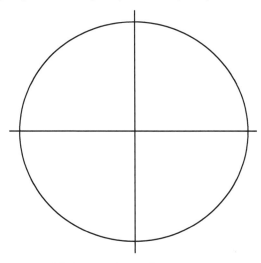

Make copies of this page

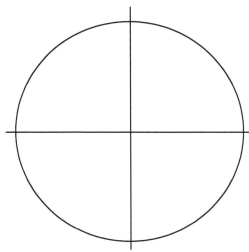

# THE TARGET

It is _mandatory_ that you see and positively identify your target before firing. After you are certain of where you will shoot, you must concentrate on the front sight only. Your attention is no longer on that target or the "X" printed on it. Instead you will position your sight alignment in the middle of the possible target.

It is imperative that you follow this technique; even though you will tend to look at the target trying to make that "perfect shot" (as you would think). You need to concentrate on the proper technique (sight alignment) instead of making your eyes look for the bullseye on the target.

> _Remember: After you achieve sight alignment, look at the front sight, not the target._

Mixon Targets

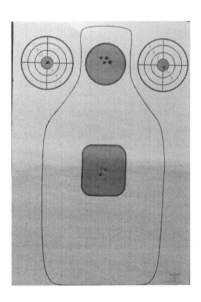

The dark areas are bright green making it easier for your eyes to identify the point of aim.

# TRIGGER CONTROL

You should squeeze the trigger using the same philosophy you use to control the pedals of your vehicle.

When you drive, you press the accelerator pedal smoothly and gradually to make the vehicle advance. If you press the pedal aggressively you might lose control of your car. Similarly, when you want to slow down, you press the brake pedal smoothly to keep control of the vehicle. Same principle applies when you drive somebody else's car; you train your legs and feet quickly to drive a different vehicle.

This principle also applies to your finger and how you should squeeze the trigger. The squeeze must be smooth and constant from the moment your finger touches the trigger. Always keep the same pressure on your trigger finger, and without hesitation press it from the beginning to the end; even if you think your sight picture is moving too much.

Trigger squeeze shall not occur until you have your sights aligned, and _you are_ focusing on the front sight; only then your trigger finger starts moving independently in a very consistent and confident motion.

> *Before you worry about shooting fast, make sure that you apply the fundamentals and that you can shoot accurately with a controlled speed.*

## Trigger Finger:

Press the trigger with the middle of the distal phalanx of your index finger *(See Fig. 23)*, which is a sensitive yet strong area of the finger. Note that you should not squeeze the trigger with the tip or the joint of the finger, which would cause your shots to impact either to the left or right of the point of impact.

Fig. 22

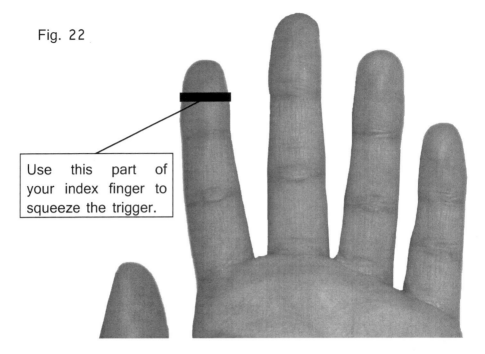

Use this part of your index finger to squeeze the trigger.

## Squeeze the Trigger:

A perfect shot happens when you squeeze the trigger with no hesitation, then your shot surprise you. You were not expecting it.

I am sure you have heard this statement several times. But do you know what "surprise" to look for? The reality is you cannot provoke this effect. Due to the finger sensibility, it is easy to know when the gun will fire, provoking anticipation of recoil, which shifts your attention from the front sight to the target. Some shooters even close their eyes (blink) just before they do the final push of the trigger.

In order to deliver a perfect shot, you must put pressure on the trigger consistently while you concentrate on the sight alignment.

Analyze your trigger control, and answer the following questions:
- Do you know exactly when the firearm is going to fire?
- Do you rush to squeeze the trigger as soon as you see that your sights pass by the "perfect" point of aim?
- Are your shot groups concentrated low and left (right-hand shooter), even if they are grouped close to the center of the target?
- After you fire, is your dominant hand red?

If you answer "yes" to most of these questions, then you definitely have trigger control issues; but don't worry, most shooters make this mistake. You can solve this by understanding that your trigger finger acts independently of your eyes.

You don't need to wait for a "perfect moment" to shoot because that moment does not exist. As soon as you have a good sight alignment, your finger starts working independently by using nonstop pressure on the trigger. By doing this, you will not anticipate the recoil or flinch; most likely your shot will surprise you.

Most of the time your first shot is good because you are concentrated on the technique and you're not expecting anything. It is your first shot, after all. The key is to repeat it over and over.

At the range, I don't want you to worry about making a perfect shot or trying to have great shot groups on the target (I know this might sound silly); instead, concentrate on trigger control and sight alignment. Even if you don't see immediate results, with more practice your shooting success will increase tremendously.

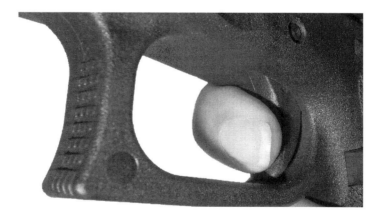

Fig. 23

Remember: You don't need to wait for a "perfect moment" to shoot because that moment does not exist.

# PRACTICE DRILLS
## Trigger Control

www.GabbyFranco.com

Perform all shooting techniques simultaneously. If you lose your front sight while aiming then, your shot won't hit the bull's-eye. The equivalent effect happens when you have a perfect sight picture but you have bad technique when you squeeze the trigger. Perfect technique is equal to perfect shot.

Exercise: Using your dominant hand, position your fingers as if you were holding the grip of a pistol (remember to keep your hand partially open). Now move the trigger finger without moving the rest of the fingers. As you see, such tasks seems simple at first, but it is not easy to do because all fingers want to move at the same time. This is something you must learn to control.
When you shoot you should move your index finger only to assure a perfect trigger control.

These are just a few simple exercises that will help you with concentration while shooting, to learn about shooting fundamentals, and to notice possible mistakes.

Spend quality time at the range by practicing perfect technique or as perfectly as possible, so your body can memorize good habits—what is known as muscle memory. Every time you shoot, you should be able to know what you did right or wrong at the moment you squeezed the trigger. If it is not clear, you must learn what went wrong by a process of elimination.
Check on possible mistakes and errors. Make notes.

# PRACTICE DRILLS
## TRIGGER CONTROL 1

Round Count: 20 rounds
Distance: 7 yards
Target: White, no bullseye or point of aim.
Shooting Hand: Dominant
Rate of Fire: Slow
Frequency: Every day at the beginning of your training session until the technique becomes natural.

During this drill, target results are important. However, you need to concentrate on perfect sight alignment and be sure to apply smooth pressure on the trigger. As explained in the trigger control chapter, your trigger squeeze must be consistent and smooth.

1. Load your pistol with 5 rounds
2. Aim at the target. While making sure you have a perfect sight alignment squeeze the trigger without hesitation.
3. Forget about the initial result on the target; trigger squeeze is smooth.
4. Be aware of your actions while shooting. Make sure your target is completely blurry and you are not anticipating your shots.
5. Target results will tell you how well (or how poorly!) you are applying the technique by analyzing where your shots are impacting the target.

Repeat this exercise until you fire 20 rounds! Make notes.

NOTES: _____

_____

_____

_____

# PRACTICE DRILLS
## TRIGGER CONTROL 2

Round Count: 10 (5 live, 5 dummy)
Distance: 7 yards
Shooting Hand: Dominant
Rapid Fire: Slow
Frequency: Every day at the beginning of your training session until the technique becomes natural.

In this exercise you will mix live rounds with dummy rounds (also called snap caps) then load your magazine without looking. As your fire, you will have snap caps between live rounds, which will show your level of anticipation.

- Your arms and body move forward when you get the dummy round. You need to reduce the pressure of your upper body muscles (shoulders, arms and trapezius muscles).

- The front sight/muzzle of the firearm moves down. You are putting too much pressure on the trigger with each shot, and you are moving all 5 fingers with the dominant hand instead of the trigger finger only.

Tell a friend (if possible) to stand behind you looking at your pistol at all times while you do this exercise. Once your pistol loads the dummy round he will be able to see if the muzzle and body moved down or not.

Repeat this exercise at least two times every day. Remember: Every shot counts. Make notes.

NOTES: _____

_____

_____

_____

_____

_____

_____

Mark or highlight your shot group to analyze your shooting technique

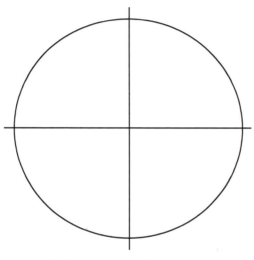

Make copies of this page

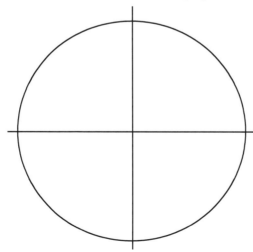

# FOLLOW-THROUGH

I know you have heard instructors, friends and enthusiastic shooters say, "You need to follow through". As a command such advice should work well; but because you pay more attention to the rest of the techniques you might have forgotten how important it is to follow through.

Most shooters want to look at the target to see where their shots landed instead of finishing the process of a shot. In order to overcome this, you need to tell your brain what you want it to do. Otherwise, your brain will work in a mechanical mode.

Even though I haven't seen you shoot, I will venture to say that you also make this mistake. There are several reasons for this:

1. You think you made your best shot and you want to make sure the bullet hit the bullseye.
2. You think it was a terrible shot so you rush to look at the target to see if you even hit it.
3. You have no clue where your shots are landing, so you are looking at the target just hoping to hit the middle of it.

The truth is the process of a shot doesn't end until you recover your front sight as if you were going to shoot again. The reason behind this is that after your brain gives your finger the command to shoot, it feels that the action already happened, which makes you lower the firearm to make room for your eyes to look at the target. As you keep doing this, your arms move faster and more aggressively—faster than your trigger finger, which creates an uncontrollable and sometimes undetected bad habit that results in shot groups low on your target.

Another important reason to follow-through: Your brain commands your eyes to keep looking at the front sight, which will help you keep them open and consecutively you will be able to call your shots.

*Remember: "the process of a shot does not end until you recover your front sight as if you were going to shoot again"*

# Mind-Set

Your brain is your computer; you create ideas, dreams, and commands that lead to your daily activities. Have you heard about dreams coming true? Well, I will substitute the word "dreams" for "commands" in this subject.

During the day, how many times do you tell yourself negative messages: "I am stupid." ... "Why did I do that?" ... "I don't want to mess up this today!" ... "I bet I will be late for work!". If you think about this for a second, you will realize that everything you tell yourself (like calling yourself "stupid" or telling yourself not to mess up) is a command, even if you don't think of it is as a big deal.

Shooting is no different. The way you behave every minute at home and work is the way you will behave (at least mentally) at the range. I am not here to make you an angel or the perfect positive person; it is your decision change for better results: Do it if you want to be more effective, at least when it comes to shooting.

I will illustrate this with a personal experience from Olympic shooting competition:

In 2002, as a member of the Venezuelan shooting team, I was competing at the South American Games in Brazil in the air pistol match. It was my last international competition as I was moving to the United States, so I decided to do my best. But most importantly, I wanted to enjoy the match. The practice session the day before was phenomenal. My coach looked at me and said, "Gabby, do not take this for granted; I want you to do tomorrow exactly what you did today." I started thinking about what I did. I had already been shooting internationally for a while, so I didn't feel any different other than I was shooting without pressure. I was not worried about my scores; I just focused on the technique. Of course that's something I should always do, but sometimes it didn't happen the way I wanted.

I started the competition relaxed and calm, and I started visualizing what I did the day before. The competition started and my shooting was very good, however, I started having doubts about what could happen. I thought, "I haven't had a bad shot yet, not even anything in the 8-ring. I bet I won't go clean in this match, but I don't want to shoot an 8." That thought took me from a perfect state of mind to a "fear of failure." I started visualizing what I did not want to happen instead of concentrating on what I wanted to happen. As expected, I made a poor shot. Only it wasn't just an 8; it landed in the 7-ring.

I was very sad and disappointed. My coach reminded me that I could not change that shot but I could work on the ones I hadn't fired yet. So I did, and I won three gold medals in that competition! The key was I was able to understand how my mind works and how sometimes it plays with me. I had to learn to control what I think, how I think and what I say to myself. Later, I will explain more about this subject, which is very critical when it comes to your shooting competitively. For now, remember: If you think about a bad shot, it will happen.

> *"...I was able to understand how my mind works and how sometimes it plays with me. I had to learn to control what I think, how I think and what I say to myself."*

## Key Points:

1. Do not think about what you don't want to happen; think about what you want to happen.
2. Encourage yourself when you make a mistake to prevent it from happening again.
3. Accept the fact that you are nervous but do not remind yourself of it.
4. Do not reinforce the error, think about the technique.
5. If your mind is busy thinking, it might as well think about something that will be beneficial for you.

# MAKING THE SHOT

Now that we have discussed the most important techniques, follow these simple steps when you shoot:

- Identify your target.

- Breathe deeply two or three times before raising your pistol. (Use you preferred breathing technique.)

- Aim at the center of the target and concentrate on the front sight.

- Let the firearm move normally. Remember, you cannot stop it from moving. You need to learn to shoot with that "constant movement."

- Trust your front sight.

- Start moving your trigger finger without stopping as you see your front sight clearly. Your target is blurry. Remember, your trigger finger must move smoothly, not aggressively.

- Forget about the perfect moment to squeeze the trigger. The perfect moment is when your front sight appears "clear" in the middle of rear sight and the target is "blurry".

- Keep your dominant eye open at all times (sometimes the blast of the pistol will make you blink).

- After you shoot, keep looking at the front sight as if you were going to make another shot, commonly known as the follow-through.

- Try not to look at your target after every shot to see where your shots are landing. Instead, do so only after you fire at least three shots in a row.

- Do not assume shooting a good group will lead to another one.

- Prepare again for another good shot by applying all the techniques.

# Dry Fire Practice

Champions consider dry fire as one of the most important practices they did during their successful career. As an Olympic shooter 60% of my training was dry firing. It was not fun, but it was effective.

Please note that you dry fire with an unloaded firearm. Snap caps or dummy rounds are commonly used to prevent damages to some firearms like rimfire pistols/rifles (ex: .22Lr pistol).

When you dry fire, do it just as if you were going to do a real shot. Your body position, hand pressure, and mind-set doesn't change. If you dry fire 1000 times without paying attention to the technique then you are developing bad muscle memory x 1000.

Tips while doing dry fire:
* Perform quality dry fire for 15 or 20 minutes a day.
* Make sure your front sight doesn't move while squeeze the trigger.
* Look at your front sight only, forget about the target or point of aim.
* From time to time perform a few dry fire with your eyes closed and concentrate on your trigger squeeze.

www.GabbyFranco.com

# RANGE CHECK LIST

- ☐ Firearm(s) you want to take to the range.

- ☐ Enough magazines for the shooting session.

- ☐ Correct ammunition for the firearm(s) you will shoot.

- ☐ Protective Gear: Eye and ear protection, etc.
  *(Page 77)*

- ☐ Shooting Gear: Belt(s), mag pouches, holster, etc.
  *(Page 78)*

- ☐ Tools and Maintenance *(Page 80)*

- ☐ Targets *(Page 80)*

- ☐ Shooting shoes

- ☐ Range/IPSC/IDPA ID card

- ☐ Cash/Check (some ranges/competitions don't take CC)

- ☐ Score sheets (competition)

- ☐ Water and snacks

- ☐ **Your shooting manual TroubleShooting (By Gabby Franco)**

# CHAPTER 3
## SHOOTING GEAR

You might be surprised how often professional shooters arrive at the range without their firearm(s) and/or gear. That's just one reason I think it is important to talk about the shooting gear and tools you should always carry in your range bag. Ensuring that you have the right equipment will not only save you time at the range, but will also make your shooting experience more enjoyable.

Besides wearing proper attire for shooting, you must take to the range items such as a hat to protect your face from hot brass. Also make sure you have the proper firearm, ammunition, and correct magazines for it. This will save you the aggravation of learning you cannot shoot once arriving at the range.

Remember that your needs might change according to the shooting activity. If you are shooting in competition, you might need certain accessories that are different from the ones you use for target practice. The same applies for hunting, tactical shooting and other disciplines. Given that fact, understand that you can change these lists according to your needs.

# PROTECTIVE GEAR

| Shooting Glasses: | |
|---|---|
| The best option is a pair of shooting glasses that cover as much of your eyes as possible. There are different colored lenses that are used depending on the light conditions of the range. | **Amber**: Work best in low light or on a cloudy day.<br><br>**Vermillion**: Excellent for shooting against green backgrounds.<br><br>**Clear**: Preferred while shooting in indoor/outdoor ranges<br><br>**Gray/Dark Gray**: Best for shooting outdoors in bright sun. |

| Hearing Protection: | |
|---|---|
| For your own benefit, always use hearing protection while shooting. | The best protection you can get comes by using ear plugs and ear muffs at the same time. Electronic ear muffs allow you to hear someone talking even in a loud indoor range. |

### Knee Pads:

Whether you shoot competitively or tactically, these will save your knees from painful bruises when kneeling on terrain covered with empty shell cases.

### Hat or Baseball Cap:

Use them while shooting because hot brass may fall in between your shooting glasses and your forehead—very painful.

# SHOOTING GEAR

## Good, Comfortable Range Bag

The best range bag you can buy is one that holds all you need but not more than what you need. Make sure you have an individual pouch that will allow you to transport your pistol from a safety table to the line of fire.

## Pistol and/or Revolver

Make sure you have the firearm(s) you want to shoot in your range bag.

## Magazines and/or Speed-Loaders

Many handguns have similar magazines but fire different calibers. Make sure the magazines you take to the range are compatible with the caliber of your pistol. Most modern pistol magazines have engraved the handgun's caliber on their sides.

The same goes for speed-loaders for revolvers: If you are going to shoot a revolver, be sure you have the right speed-loaders for it.

If you like to shoot a magazine-fed pistol a lot or if loading several magazines in one session is not your favorite part of shooting, buy a magazine speed-loader, which will help you load cartridges a lot faster and easier. It will also save your thumbs.

## Holster, Belt, Mag Pouches/Speed-Loader Holders

Similarly, a holster might be used for several different firearms but not every model on the market. If you own different models of firearms, make sure you have the proper holster in your range bag before you leave home.

# SHOOTING GEAR

## Correct Ammunition for Your Firearm(s)

Don't forget to carry the correct ammunition for your pistol. When purchasing ammo, be sure to ask for the correct load.

Some common pitfalls:
9x19 is commonly called 9mm but it's also known as: 9mm Luger, 9x19mm, and 9mm Parabellum;
9x18 is commonly known as 9mm Makarov and 9x18mm PM;
9X17 is commonly known as .380 ACP, 9mm Short, 9mm Browning, and 9mm Kurtz.

## Chair

This is a suggestion. If you are shooting on an outdoor range, take with you a small but comfortable chair so you can rest when you are not shooting.

## Targets

- Take enough targets for your shooting session.
- Have pasters on hand to cover your shots on the targets.
- Highly recommended: www.mixontargets.com

## Practice Equipment

-Dummy Rounds
-Timer

# Tool and Cleaning Equipment

## Small Cleaning Kit

Always carry in your range bag a small bottle of gun oil and brushes.

## Rod

In case a bullet gets stuck inside the barrel (a squib load)

## Allen Keys, Punches, Screw Drivers

Always have compatible Allen keys to your firearm(s) and optics. Flat-head screw drivers can also help clear certain malfunctions. Most modern firearms are disassembled with a punch, which will be useful if you need to take apart your gun.

## Pocketknife or Multi-tool

Who doesn't like one? Extremely versatile with a wide variety of uses.

## Magazine Brush

Commonly used by USPSA shooters. If you are dropping your magazines in the dirt, you might want to clean them to maximize their performance and avoid malfunctions.

# CHAPTER 4
## CHOOSE THE RIGHT FIREARM

Purchasing the right handgun for a specific purpose might seem difficult and confusing at first. I'm sure you've read gun magazines, searched the Internet, read articles, checked out pistols at the gun shop, and maybe even rented them at the range. And yet you still have doubts. You aren't sure which one you should buy. To clarify all the questions and concerns you have, I will give you a simple but very helpful guide of how to narrow all the choices of firearms and how to choose one that fits you best.

## FIRST - DETERMINE PURPOSE OF USE.

### Concealed Carry or Tactical Shooting

Consider the size and the possible ways you might carry the handgun(s). It is very important that you get suggestions from friends, instructors, and experts about the different firearms, calibers, sizes, etc. But before you make your final decision consider the following:

- Where will you carry the handgun? (IWB, OWB, Ankle, purse, fanny pack, etc.)

- Body size (Will it be comfortable for you to carry a full-size handgun?)
- Clothes (Will you be able to cover the pistol with the clothes you normally wear?)
- Accessibility (Will you be able to draw your gun fast enough from the ankle holster?)

These are some of the important questions you should ask yourself before you go to a gun shop to buy a firearm. Know your needs before you buy.

## Competitive Shooting and Target Practice

Shooting, like many other sports, has different disciplines in which you can use the same type of firearm you would use for self-defense. Become familiar with the different types of competitions available and the types of firearms allowed by the rules of each discipline. If you just want a handgun for target practice then search for a full size handgun as these will be the most accurate models.

Here is a list of the different disciplines of shooting with their websites:

### Target shooting and Olympic shooting

- http://www.issf-sports.org/
  ISSF (Int'l Shooting Sport Federation)

- http://www.usashooting.org/
  Olympic Shooting (USA Shooting)

- http://competitions.nra.org/how-to-get-started.aspx
  NRA Competitions

- http://www.teamusa.org/USA-Modern-Pentathlon.aspx
  Modern Pentathlon

- http://www.thecmp.org/
  Bullseye shooting at Camp Perry, OH

## Practical Shooting

- http://uspsa.com/
  USPSA (US Practical Shooting Association)

- http://www.ipsc.org/
  IPSC (Int'l Practical Shooting Confederation)

- http://www.3gunnation.com/
  3gun/Multi-gun competition

- http://www.idpa.com/
  IDPA - Int'l Defensive Pistol Association

## Other handgun competitions

- http://www.ihmsa.org/
  Int'l Handgun Metallic Silhouette Association

- http://www.actionairgun.com/learn.php
  Action Airgun

- http://www.sassnet.com
  SASS (Single Action Shooting Society)

Please note that these are just a small list of the web sites with competition information. Feel free to contact your gun club and ask for local and national competitions.

# Second — Choose The Right Caliber

Choosing a manageable caliber is critical. This doesn't necessarily mean that you can't shoot some of the more powerful firearms but choosing a caliber that *you* can comfortably shoot allows you to keep the concentration in the technique without thinking on the recoil.

I recommend mastering the proper technique before moving to a high recoil cartridge.

# Third — Consider The Ergonomics And Your Hand Size

The techniques I teach will help you apply the fundamentals of shooting in a way that you can shoot accurately with any firearm you put in your hands. However, to master the shooting technique through perfect repetition whether for concealed carry, competition, tactical, or precision shooting it is very important to choose a handgun with a grip that fits your hand.

Example: A shooter with a wide palm and short fingers might not feel comfortable shooting a full size pistol with a large grip; in the other hand, a shooter with longer fingers will feel more comfortable shooting that same pistol.

*"Having the right firearm for you will increase your shooting results and your accuracy."*
*- Gabby Franco*

www.GabbyFranco.com

www.GabbyFranco.com

86

# CHAPTER 5
## TROUBLESHOOTING

Often shooters try to perfect technique by fixing errors according to what they see on a target, either by compensating or by changing parts and adjusting sights without first fixing the main problem: Technique. But shooting, like any other sport, demands proper technique. Even when you have learned proper technique, you may find yourself making mistakes. It is critical to detected and rectify these errors as soon as possible to avoid developing bad habits.

Let's take a look at some of the most common questions to help you find a possible solution to some shooting mistakes. Note that it is impossible to cover all questions; however, I will address more questions and answers in future editions.

# Shooting Stance

Learning to understand what your body is telling you is very important. If something doesn't feel right it's because it is not right. If you're in pain, or get tired very quickly it is because you are not maximizing your efforts. While you're shooting, you must also pay attention to everything else other than the trigger and the sight alignment—your hands, your feet, your legs, etc.

### I feel that I am not recovering my front sight fast enough, and my toes are moving up every time I fire.
This is a shooting position problem, sometimes shooters shoot with their back straight and legs fully extended.

- You need to check whether your knees are slightly bent. Verify that your chest is forward and relax your upper body muscles.

### I keep my chest forward but my toes are still moving up every time I fire. *See page 32*
Perhaps you are trying to put your chest forward as I have explained previously, but you are forgetting about your knees.

- Check whether your legs are straight; if they are, bend them slightly. Keep your chest in balance with the rest of your body, make sure you are not pushing your chest too far forward.

### Every time I shoot the thumb of my dominant hand hurts. *See page 40, Fig. 18.*
This happen when you have a bad grip and most likely your trigger finger is extended too far forward.

- Make sure you have a correct grip with your dominant hand. The pistol might be too wide for your hand and so the recoil of the pistol is hitting the muscle of your thumb only.

## I am a cross-dominant shooter (right-handed, left eye-dominant). *See page 21, Fig. 2*

1. Move the pistol and align the sights with your dominant eye; the pistol adapts to you, no otherwise.
2. Do not rotate your face; hold it in a normal position facing the target.
3. Keep your body square to the target.

## My dominant hand is red after shooting a couple of rounds.

You are putting too much pressure on the pistol grip.
   - Relax your dominant hand; it might be too tight.
   Remember that your support hand should control the majority of the pressure over the pistol. Your dominant hand's job is to squeeze the trigger.

## When I put my chest forward my lower back hurts.

You want to apply the technique as explained, however you need to do it according to your physical ability.
Some shooters may use a more aggressive position than others. Bending your knees a little is better than nothing.
   - Check if you are bending the knee too much, almost like doing a squat. You must bend the knees to a comfortable position. Also, make sure your chest is forward enough for you to control the recoil but not too much that cause discomfort while shooting.

# FRONT SIGHT

If you want to do a perfect shot, then you better look at the front sight. The front sight is like the steering wheel of your vehicle: wherever the steering wheel points the vehicle will go, and wherever the front sight points the shot will go. While you are driving you make sure that your steering wheel is straight and not drifting left-and-right so the vehicle doesn't sway from side to side on the road.

You must apply same philosophy with your front sight. Make sure it's completely aligned and clear in your vision.

---

**I cannot see my front sight clear, sometimes it is blurry. Answer these questions:** *See page 50, Fig. 20*

- Do you have problems seeing objects at short distance?
  If so, you need to use your prescription lenses to see the front sight. If you have no problems seeing objects at short distance, most likely you are looking at the target instead of the front sight.
  Remember: the target must be blurry at all times.

- Are you using prescription lenses to see objects, like the target, at distance? If so, that is why you don't see the front sight clearly. If you do not use prescription lenses to see objects at distance, be sure you are focusing on the front sight. Sometimes your eyes switch between your target and your front sight. Make sure this is not your case.

- Do you shoot with your chin tucked in on your shooting position? If the answer is "yes," maybe the border of your lenses are interfering with your vision. Also, by looking at an angle you lose your peripheral vision, and it will be harder to focus on the front sight. If the answer is "no", refer to the previous answers.

## I see the front sight clearly but I still don't fire a good shot group.

The fact that you see the front sight doesn't mean that you are actually "focusing" on it. You could be looking at it for minutes if you wanted to, but the key is to maintain the concentration and keep looking at the front sight until the end of the process of your shot.

## When I shoot I see that my front sight moves down.

You might be pressing the trigger too aggressively or putting pressure in all finger when you squeeze the trigger. The best way to fix this issue is by doing dry fire and watching your front sight movement while pressing the trigger. Press the trigger with the middle of the distal phalanx of your index finger *(Check page 61 and 73)*.

## When I shoot my front sight is moving up.

This is happening because you are anticipating your shots by exaggerating the natural movement of your gun after it fires. Too much tension on your upper body increases your anticipation after each shot.
- Relax your upper body muscles. More importantly you need to forget about the recoil of the firearm, which might be subconsciously scaring you.

## When I raise my pistol, my sights are not aligned (front sight points left or right).

Right-hand shooter: Make sure you have a proper grip. If your front sight is on the right you likely have too much finger toward the trigger.

Left-hand shooter: If your front sight is on the left, then there is too little finger on your trigger and your hand is not properly placed.

# TRIGGER CONTROL

Shooting is similar to a mathematical equation: You won't have a good result if the equation is not done perfectly. In shooting, you won't hit the bullseye if you only concentrate your attention on the front sight and your stance, but you forget about the trigger squeeze.
You must apply all techniques simultaneously.

It might look easy to squeeze a trigger because moving a finger is something anybody can do. However, your finger has muscles that normally work together with the rest of the fingers.

To do a perfect shot, you must learn how to isolate your index finger from the rest of your hand while squeezing the trigger. Learn how to use the muscle of your finger to put the perfect amount of pressure to the trigger, as you would teach any muscle of your body how to lift weights. Just because it looks simple doesn't mean it is simple.

### I have a compact pistol, and sometimes it is difficult for me to squeeze the trigger all the way to the rear.
Most likely you don't have a good grip. Make sure that your grip is in-line with your hand and arm as shown on page 40. Remember to Press the trigger with the middle of the distal phalanx of your index finger. *(Check page 61).*

### I pressed the trigger but bullet didn't go off. I think I didn't squeeze the trigger all the way to the rear. Why did it happen?
Most likely you're applying the so-called "death grip," which means you are putting too much pressure on the pistol with your dominant hand. When you apply too much pressure, your finger won't release the trigger correctly allowing it to travel fully and reset.
Relax your dominant hand and shoot again.

# Shooting Impacts

Most shooters only see holes in a target; they only care to see if they shoot good or bad or whether most of their shots are close to the bullseye or not. A target tells you more than that. To understand the placement of each shot and why it happens, you need to learn how to read and analyze a target.

---

**Right-handed shooter: All my shots are low and to the left of the bullseye.**
**Left-handed shooter: All my shots are low and to the right of the bullseye.**

- Make sure you have a good grip and that you're using the middle of the distal phalanx of your index finger. *(Check page 62).*
- Pay attention to the way you are pressing the trigger, it seems like you are jerking the trigger.
- Check to see if you are putting too much pressure on the pistol with your dominant hand. Also, be sure you are looking and focusing on the front sight until the pistol fires.
- Sometimes we are too quick for our own good. Before you press the trigger you could be shifting your focus from the front sight to the target, which won't keep a good sight alignment. Such movement can occur so quickly that it is impossible for the shooter to recognize he/she is doing it. Sometimes it's hard for someone else to notice it, too, but your best bet is to ask a friend to watch you as you shoot.

Bottom line: If you don't know where the front sight moved when you pressed the trigger, then you were not looking at the front sight. Lastly, are you provoking your shots? Do you know exactly when your pistol will fire? If you answered "yes" to either question, you are anticipating your shots and creating resistance to the recoil of the pistol.

### I have very good trigger control but my shots are still scattered around the bullseye. *See page 68.*

Most likely you are losing the front sight at the moment you pull the trigger.

Ask yourself: Am I looking at the front sight? Is the target blurry? Remember to look at the front sight until the end of the process of your shot, which will guarantee perfect shots. You need a good trigger control to hit the bullseye as well.

---

### All my shots are landing in a specific area on the target away from the bullseye.

This is a typical sight alignment issue. Is your sight alignment perfect? The top of your front sight must be perfectly aligned with the top of your rear sight.

The best way to verify if the sights need to be adjusted is by shooting supported on the shooting table. Shoot at least 3 shots with perfect technique (*perfect sight picture and perfect trigger control*). Ask a friend you know is a good shooter to do the same. Then you can compare these results with your previous target to confirm whether the error was caused by you or the firearm.

Adjust the rear sight only if, after firing three perfect shots (supported on a bench), you determine the sights are off (good elevation but bad windage), meaning the gun may have been dropped previously or the sights bumped, causing them to drift from their previous adjustment.

If the shots are in the middle of the target, the problem is not the sights but your technique.

---

### Should I adjust my stance and grip every time I have a bad shot?

No. Even though it is likely the bad shot was caused by you, don't readjust every single time. Before you start firing, be sure of your position, your grip, and the rest of the technique.

Before you readjust after a bad shot, fire three more rounds to confirm the first one wasn't a fluke. If all three land in the same area then you can readjust according to the confirmed error. Shooting is all about consistency. You cannot be consistent if you change everything you're doing after each round.

## My shooting group is too wide at 7 yards.

There are too many reason for this to happen: You could be losing your front sight at the moment you squeeze the trigger, your trigger squeeze is too aggressive, you have too much tension on your upper body muscles, etc.

You need to read through the book from the beginning, and start learning proper shooting technique. Shooting is more than just perfect trigger squeeze. Proper technique includes how to position yourself, align your sights, and perfect trigger squeeze—those factors are mandatory if you want to shoot better and better.

# Mind-Set

Your brain is just like a computer: You need to give it commands for action. If you don't, your brain will act by itself. All the information learned is in your brain, stored in a specific file and ready to use upon request. But it's up to you to reach for that available information at any time by requesting it. How do you request this information? Basically, you must think about the subject in question.

Think about the front sight and automatically your brain will start looking for the information; most likely you will start thinking how clear you must see the front sight and how the target must stay blurry on your vision.

Be aware of your thoughts, whether they are positive, negative or if they are effective. A shooter thinks, "I don't want to shoot badly." In this case, a shooter may believe that this was a positive thought because he/she was avoiding a bad shot with imagination. But the reality is the shooter is increasing the fear of a bad shot by thinking about it. Just think about this for a second. You cannot fix something that is not wrong in the first place. The shooter in the above scenario is picturing a bad shot instead of picturing perfect technique.

---

### I fear long shots because I normally don't shoot at great distances; when I do results are not so good.

The only way to overcome fear is to understand it. Technique doesn't change whether you are shooting at 3, 7, or 25 yards you must apply the same technique.

If you need to think about something, think about something that will help—think about technique instead of thinking how bad you shot last time at that specific distance. Think that you are shooting at a smaller target instead of thinking that your target is far away.

Play with your mind for your own benefit.

## Do I have to think about something while shooting?

You don't have to, but in practice it will help develop muscle memory to revise technique before you shoot. Thinking about the technique doesn't mean you will over-think it. Normally, you think about it before you fire. While you are shooting, your body will repeat what you have practiced.

## I always think I want to make a good shot.

Thinking of making a good shot is good but it's not enough. Think about *technique* and how it must be performed.

# GLOSSARY

**Anticipating the recoil**
Shooter knows when the firearm will fire and so expects the gun to recoil causing him to instinctively move the wrist up or down.

**Distal Phalanx**
Bone located at the tip of the digits of your fingers and toes.

**Dummy Rounds**
Is an inert round that lets you simulate firearms malfunctions, and can be used to dry fire, test the feeding, extraction of your pistol or rifle.

**Electronic ear muffs**
Ear protection designed to amplify weak noises while blocking loud noises.

**IDPA**
International Defensive Pistol Association

**IWB / OWB**
Inside the waistband / outside the waistband.

**Limp-wristing**
Commonly happens with semi-auto pistols, where the shooter doesn't have a firm grip and the pistol fails to complete the operating cycle.

**Magazine**
Feeding devise and ammunition storage used with pistols and rifles.

**Magazine speed-loader**
Helps you load pistol or rifle magazines quickly and easier without pinching your fingers.

**Marksman**
A person who is skilled in precision with a firearm such as with a

handgun and/or rifle.

## Marksmanship
The art or skill to use a firearm proficiently.

## Natural point of aim
Perfect point where your body is naturally aligned with your target.

## Olympic Shooting
Olympic sport that includes the use of rifles, pistols and shotguns of different calibers. Check: http://www.issf-sports.org/

## Pan-American Games
Major event in the Americas in which athletes compete in a variety of summer sport competitions.

## Prone Position
Shooting position in which the shooter is facing down laying on the ground; this a great position to obtain stability while shooting at long distances.

## Range
Indoor or outdoor facility design for the use of firearms.

## Recoil
Commonly known as the kickback movement that happens after a gun is fired.

## Reload/Handloading
A way shooters may safe significant amount of money by producing their own ammunition using special machinery and components.

## Tactical shooting
Someone shooting practices are based into realistic shooting stages to develop the skills to survive a life threatening situation.

## USPSA
United States Practical Shooting Association. http://uspsa.com/

Made in the USA
San Bernardino, CA
16 August 2013